Copy That Converts

The Art and Science of Writing Ad Copy
Jules Beshears

Copyright © 2023 by Jules Beshears / 414 Industries

All rights reserved.

No portion of this book may be reproduced in any form without written permission from the publisher or author, except as permitted by U.S. copyright law.

Message From The Author

"Iwas told we are paid for our value and not our time." As such, my books, on the surface, may seem somewhat lacking in terms of page count. What they lack in the sheer number of pages that tell stories about me growing up, or making my first million, etc., I choose to prioritize value. The books I write remove most of the fluff and are condensed, distilled, raw value that will hopefully change your life for the better.

This book is dedicated to my family, friends, and to all the entrepreneurs that chose never to give up.

Contents

1. Introduction to Ad Copywriting 1
2. Understanding Your Target Audience 3
3. The Art of Crafting a Headline 6
4. The Importance of a Unique Value Proposition 9
5. Writing Body Copy that Converts 12
6. Creating a Call to Action that Gets Results 15
7. Using Emotion to Sell Products 18
8. Writing Effective Social Media Ad Copy 21
9. Writing Effective Social Media Ad Copy 23
10. Measuring the Success of Your Ad Copy 26
11. Tips and Tricks for Writing Ad Copy That Works 29
12. Conclusion and Final Thoughts on Ad Copywriting 31

1.
2.
3.
4.
5.
6.
7.
8.
9.
10.
11.

Chapter 1

Introduction to Ad Copywriting

Ad copywriting is the art and science of writing effective advertisements. It is crafting words and messages that sell products and services. As consumers are bombarded with hundreds, if not thousands, of promotions daily, ad copywriting is a critical skill for businesses looking to stand out and make an impact.

Ad copywriting is a multi-disciplinary field that combines elements of marketing, psychology, and writing. A good ad copywriter must have a deep understanding of the target audience, a sharp eye for detail, and an ability to craft compelling messages that resonate with the target audience.

At its core, ad copywriting is about understanding the needs, desires, and motivations of the target audience and then using that understanding to craft messages that speak directly to them. Whether it's a headline, body copy, or a call to action, every word in an advertisement must work together to achieve a specific goal – to get the target audience to take action.

We will dive into the fundamentals of ad copywriting and explore the key elements that make a great advertisement. We will examine the role of research and audience analysis, the importance of a strong headline, the power of a unique value proposition, and the art of crafting body copy that converts.

Ad copywriting is a constantly evolving field, and as new technologies emerge, so do new opportunities for advertisers. For example, with the rise of social media and e-commerce, ad copywriting has become increasingly crucial for businesses looking to reach new customers and sell products online. Advertisers must understand the unique challenges and opportunities presented by different media formats and be able to adjust their ad copy accordingly.

In addition to writing compelling ad copy, it is also essential to measure the success of your advertisements. This requires tracking key metrics such as clicks, conversions, and engagement and using the data to continually improve your ad copywriting skills.

One of the biggest challenges of ad copywriting is standing out in a crowded marketplace. With so many advertisements vying for consumers' attention, it's essential to be creative and think outside the box. This requires understanding what makes your product or service unique and using that knowledge to create ads that stand out from the crowd.

Ad copywriting is not just about writing advertisements – it's about understanding your target audience, crafting messages that resonate with them, and using those messages to drive results. Whether you're advertising a product or service, you must deeply understand your target audience and the messages that will resonate with them.

Ad copywriting is a critical skill for businesses of all sizes. By understanding the fundamentals of ad copywriting, companies can create advertisements that stand out from the crowd, drive results, and build lasting relationships with their target audience.

Chapter 2

Understanding Your Target Audience

The foundation of effective ad copywriting is a deep understanding of your target audience. This means knowing who they are, what they want, and what motivates them. To write ad copy that resonates with your target audience and drives results, it is essential to have a deep understanding of their needs, desires, and motivations.

To begin, it is crucial to define your target audience. This includes creating detailed demographic and psychographic profiles that include age, gender, education level, income, and interests. The more you know about your target audience, the better equipped you will be to create advertisements that speak directly to them.

Once you have defined your target audience, it is important to conduct market research to understand their needs, desires, and motivations. This can include surveys, focus groups, and interviews with target audience members. The information gathered from this research will be instrumental in shaping the messaging and tone of your advertisements.

It is also essential to understand the different ways in which your target audience consumes media. For example, are they more likely to be reached through social media, email, or direct mail? Are they more likely to respond to short-form or long-form advertisements? Understanding these nuances can help you make informed decisions about the format and channel for your advertisements.

In addition to understanding your target audience's needs, desires, and motivations, it is also essential to understand their pain points and challenges. What are the obstacles they face in their daily lives? What are the problems they are trying to solve? Understanding these pain points can help you craft advertisements that speak directly to the needs of your target audience and offer solutions to their challenges.

Moreover, understanding your target audience can also help you create more targeted and personalized advertisements. Personalization has become increasingly important in advertising, as consumers are likelier to engage with ads tailored to their specific needs and interests. Using the information gathered from your market research, you can create advertisements that speak directly to your target audience's individual needs and desires.

It is also important to regularly review and update your understanding of your target audience, as their needs and desires may change over time. This may be due to changes in their circumstances, the introduction of new products or services, or shifts in the marketplace. By staying up-to-date with changes in your target audience, you can ensure that your advertisements remain relevant and effective.

In addition, it is essential to consider the values and beliefs of your target audience when writing ad copy. For example, are they environmentally conscious? Do they prioritize health and wellness? Understanding these values and beliefs can help you create advertisements that align with the principles and values of your target audience.

Finally, it is vital to be aware of cultural and language differences when writing ad copy. This is especially important for businesses that operate in multiple countries or regions. It is essential to understand each target audience's cultural norms and values and to tailor your advertisements accordingly. For example, the language and tone used in advertisements in the US may differ from those used in Asia or Europe.

Understanding your target audience is critical to effective ad copywriting. By deeply understanding their needs, desires, motivations, pain points, and values, you can write advertisements that speak directly to your target audience and drive results. Regularly reviewing and updating your understanding of your target audience will ensure that your advertisements remain relevant and effective over time.

Chapter 3

The Art of Crafting a Headline

The headline is the first and often the most critical aspect of an advertisement. It is the first thing a reader sees and is often the determining factor as to whether or not they will continue reading. As such, compelling and attention-grabbing headlines are vital to effective ad copywriting.

There are several elements to consider when crafting a headline, including length, tone, and language. A headline should be short, concise, and to the point, typically no more than 10-12 words. It should also be attention-grabbing and make a bold statement that motivates the reader to continue reading.

In terms of tone, the headline should be appropriate for the target audience and align with the overall tone of the advertisement. For example, a headline for a serious or business-oriented advertisement should have a professional tone, while a headline for a more lighthearted or fun advertisement can be more playful.

The language used in the headline should also be carefully considered. The headline should be easy to read and understand and use simple, clear language that is easily comprehended by the target audience. Avoid using complex jargon or technical terms, as the reader may not understand these.

In addition to these basic elements, several headline formats are commonly used in advertisements, including:

- Question headlines: These headlines pose a question relevant to the target audience, such as "Are you tired of feeling exhausted all the time?"
- Statement headlines: These headlines make a bold statement relevant to the target audience, such as "Discover the secret to a better life."
- How-to headlines: These headlines offer a solution to a problem faced by the target audience, such as "How to lose weight without dieting."
- List headlines: These headlines present a list of benefits or features of a product or service, such as "5 reasons to choose our product."

The headline should also be optimized for search engines if the advertisement will be displayed online. This means including relevant keywords and phrases commonly searched for by the target audience.

It's also important to remember the context in which the advertisement will be displayed. For example, if the ad is to be displayed on social media, the headline should be optimized for the platform's character count limitations. If it is displayed on a website, the headline should be designed to complement the overall design and layout of the page.

Another consideration is the emotional impact of the headline. The headline should be written to elicit an emotional response from the reader, such as excitement, curiosity, or fear. Emotional headlines tend to be more memorable and effective as they resonate with the reader on a deeper level.

Finally, testing different headlines is a crucial step in the headline-writing process. This can be done through A/B testing, where two different headlines are tested to see which is more effective. This can also help you determine which headline format works best for your target audience and which language and tone resonate most with them.

It's also important to remember the context in which the advertisement will be displayed. For example, if the advertisement is to be displayed on social media, the headline should be optimized for the platform's character count limitations. If it is displayed on a website, the headline should be designed to complement the overall design and layout of the page.

Another consideration is the emotional impact of the headline. The headline should be written in a way that elicits an emotional response from the reader, such as excitement, curiosity, or fear. Emotional headlines tend to be more memorable and effective as they resonate with the reader on a deeper level.

Finally, testing different headlines is a crucial step in the headline-writing process. This can be done through A/B testing, where two different headlines are tested to see which is more effective. This can also help you determine which headline format works best for your target audience and which language and tone resonate most with them.

In conclusion, the art of crafting a headline is a critical component of ad copywriting. By considering elements such as length, tone, language, format, search engine optimization, context, emotional impact, and testing, you can write headlines that are attention-grabbing, memorable, and effective in driving results.

Chapter 4

The Importance of a Unique Value Proposition

A unique value proposition (UVP) is a clear and concise statement that defines the unique benefits and value a product or service offers the customer. It is a critical component of effective ad copywriting, as it helps to differentiate the product or service from its competitors and clearly communicate why the customer should choose it over other options.

A UVP should be centered around the customer and what they stand to gain from using the product or service. This means focusing on the unique features and benefits the product or service offers and the problem it solves for the customer. It should also be concise and easy to understand, typically no more than a few sentences.

Having a strong UVP is important for several reasons. Firstly, it helps to establish the product or service as a leader in its category, differentiating it from its competitors and making it more appealing to the customer. Secondly, it helps to focus the customer's attention on the key benefits and value that the product or service offers, making it easier for them to make a purchasing decision.

In addition to these benefits, a UVP can also help drive results, as it is a vital component of the overall marketing and advertising strategy. By focusing on the unique benefits and value that the product or service offers, the UVP helps to drive interest and engagement, leading to increased conversions and sales.

When crafting a UVP, it is essential to focus on the customer and what they stand to gain from using the product or service. This means considering their needs, wants, and pain points and crafting a UVP that addresses these issues and provides a clear solution.

It's also important to ensure that the rest of the advertisement, including the headline, body copy, and call to action, supports the UVP. The UVP should be a consistent theme throughout the advertisement, helping reinforce the unique benefits and value that the product or service offers the customer.

It's also important to regularly review and update the UVP to ensure that it remains relevant and effective. This may involve re-evaluating the target audience, researching competitors, and monitoring industry trends and advancements. Updating the UVP helps to ensure that it continues to resonate with the target audience and effectively communicates the unique benefits and value of the product or service.

In terms of tone and language, the UVP should be written in a way that appeals to the target audience. This may involve using language and terminology that they are familiar with and a tone that is engaging and persuasive. It's also essential to keep the UVP concise and easy to understand, avoiding complex jargon and technical language.

When creating a UVP, it's important to focus on the specific benefits and value of the product or service rather than simply listing features. Features are important, but they should be framed in terms of the benefits that they provide to the customer. For example, a component such as "advanced security features" can be framed as a benefit such as "keeping your personal information safe and secure."

Finally, using the UVP in all of the product's or service's marketing materials, including websites, advertisements, brochures, and email campaigns, is important. This helps to ensure consistency and reinforces the unique benefits and value of the product or service.

Creating a unique value proposition is a critical step in effective ad copywriting. By focusing on the target audience and their needs, researching competitors and industry trends, and making the UVP a consistent theme throughout all marketing materials, you can create a UVP that effectively communicates the unique benefits and value of the product or service and drives results.

Chapter 5

Writing Body Copy that Converts

The body copy is the main content of an advertisement, and its primary purpose is to reinforce the message of the headline and provide more detailed information about the product or service being advertised. The body copy should be written to engage the reader, convince them of the product or service's value, and ultimately compel them to take action.

Here are some tips for writing body copy that converts:

1. Keep it short and sweet: The body copy should be concise and to the point, avoiding unnecessary words or information that does not directly relate to the product or service being advertised.

2. Focus on benefits: The body copy should focus on the product or service's benefits rather than just its features. For example, instead of saying, "Our product has a long battery life," the body copy could say, "Stay powered all day with our long-lasting battery."

3. Use storytelling: Storytelling is a powerful tool in advertising, as it helps to engage the reader and make the product or service more relatable. Consider using anecdotes, case studies, or customer testimonials to demonstrate the product's or service's benefits.

4. Highlight unique features: If the product or service has unique features that set it apart from its competitors, these should be highlighted in the body copy. For example, "Our product is

the only one on the market that includes X feature, which means Y benefit for you."

5. Make it easy to read: The body copy should be easy to read and understand, using clear, concise language and short paragraphs. This makes it more likely that the reader will engage with the content and take action.
6. Use images: Images are a powerful tool in advertising and can help to reinforce the message of the body copy. Consider including images that help to demonstrate the benefits of the product or service, such as product shots, illustrations, or photographs.
7. Test and iterate: Finally, it's crucial to regularly test and refine the body copy to ensure that it is effective and converting. This may involve conducting A/B tests, collecting customer feedback, or using data analysis to track performance.
8. Use persuasive language: The body copy should use compelling language that convinces the reader of the product's or service's value. This may involve using words that evoke emotions, such as "reliable," "affordable," "convenient," "safe," etc. It may also involve using language that makes the reader feel they need to take advantage of the offered product or service.
9. Create a sense of urgency: Creating a sense of urgency can be a powerful motivator for the reader to take action. This may involve using language that implies that the opportunity is limited, such as "limited time only," "while supplies last," "limited edition," etc. It may also involve emphasizing the

benefits of taking action now, such as "take advantage of this opportunity now and enjoy X benefit."

10. Call to action: The body copy should include a clear and compelling call to action, such as "Buy now," "Sign up today," "Get started," etc. This should be positioned in a prominent location and written in a way that is easy to understand and follow.
11. Personalization: Personalizing the body copy can help to increase engagement and conversion rates. This may involve using the reader's name, location, or other relevant information, such as "Get started with X today and join the thousands of other people in Y who are enjoying Z benefit."
12. Mobile optimization: With more and more people accessing the internet via mobile devices, optimizing the body copy for mobile viewing is essential. This may involve using smaller font sizes, shorter paragraphs, and larger call-to-action buttons that are easy to tap on a small screen.

Writing body copy that converts requires careful consideration of the target audience, the product or service being advertised, and the overall message and tone of the advertisement. By focusing on benefits, using persuasive language, creating a sense of urgency, including a clear call to action, personalizing the content, and optimizing for mobile viewing, you can create body copy that effectively communicates the value of the product or service and compels the reader to take action.

Chapter 6

Creating a Call to Action that Gets Results

A call to action (CTA) is a crucial element in any advertising copy, as it is the part that encourages the reader to take action. A well-crafted CTA can make the difference between a successful ad campaign and one that falls flat. In this chapter, we will explore the critical elements of a successful CTA and provide tips for creating CTAs that get results.

1. Be clear and concise: The CTA should be clear and concise so that the reader knows precisely what action they are being asked to take. Avoid using vague language or confusing phrases, as this will decrease the chances of the reader taking action. Instead, use clear and concise language that is easy to understand, such as "Sign up now" or "Buy now."

2. Make it prominent: The CTA should be positioned in a prominent location near the headline or at the end of the body copy. This will make it more visible to the reader and increase the chances of them taking action.

3. Emphasize the benefits: The CTA should emphasize the benefits of taking the desired action. This could include getting a discount, a free trial, or access to exclusive content. The reader will be more motivated to take action by highlighting the benefits.

4. Use action-oriented language: The CTA should use action-oriented language that inspires the reader to take immediate

action. This may include using verbs such as "get," "start," "join," or "sign up."
5. Make it personal: Personalizing the CTA can help to increase its effectiveness. This may involve using the reader's name, location, or other relevant information, such as "Get started with X today and join the thousands of other people in Y who are enjoying Z benefit."
6. Test and optimize: Finally, it's important to test and optimize the CTA to ensure it is as effective as possible. This may involve testing different versions of the CTA, using different language, or positioning it in different locations within the ad.
7. Make it urgent: Adding a sense of urgency to the CTA can increase its effectiveness. This could involve using language such as "limited time only" or "act now." Urgency can create a sense of scarcity and motivate the reader to take action immediately.
8. Keep it simple: The CTA should be simple and straightforward so that the reader knows exactly what they need to do. Avoid using complex or confusing language, as this will decrease the chances of the reader taking action.
9. Use contrasting colors: The CTA should stand out from the rest of the ad by using contrasting colors. This will draw the reader's attention to the CTA and increase its visibility.
10. Make it specific: The CTA should be specific and direct so that the reader knows exactly what they need to do. For example, instead of using "Learn more" as a CTA, use "Sign up for our newsletter" or "Download our free guide."

11. Use active verbs: The CTA should use active verbs that inspire the reader to take action. This may include using verbs such as "click," "Subscribe," "download," or "register."
12. Track and analyze results: Finally, it's important to track and analyze the results of your CTAs to understand their effectiveness. This may involve using tools such as Google Analytics, heat mapping software, or A/B testing to understand how the CTA performs and identify improvement areas.

By keeping the CTA clear and concise, emphasizing the benefits, using action-oriented language, personalizing the content, adding a sense of urgency, making it simple, using contrasting colors, making it specific, using active verbs, and continually tracking and analyzing the results, you can create CTAs that are effective and drive conversions for your business.

Chapter 7

Using Emotion to Sell Products

Emotions play a crucial role in decision-making and can be leveraged to increase the effectiveness of ad campaigns. By tapping into the target audience's emotions, advertisers can create a strong connection with the reader and drive conversions. In this chapter, we will explore the role of emotion in advertising and provide tips for using emotion to sell products.

1. Know your audience: The first step in using emotion to sell products is understanding the target audience. This involves researching the target audience's values, beliefs, pain points, and emotional triggers. By understanding the target audience, advertisers can create ads that resonate emotionally with the reader.

2. Identify the right emotions: The next step is identifying the right ones to target. This may involve tapping into emotions such as happiness, fear, excitement, or inspiration. Advertisers should choose emotions that align with the product and the target audience.

3. Use storytelling: Storytelling is a powerful tool for evoking emotions in advertising. By using storytelling techniques, such as characters, plot, and setting, advertisers can connect with the reader and tap into their emotions.

4. Use visuals: Visuals, such as images and videos, can also be used to evoke emotions in advertising. Advertisers should choose visuals that align with the target audience and the

desired emotions and that are high-quality and attention-grabbing.
5. Use language that resonates: The language used in the ad copy should resonate emotionally with the reader. This may involve using language that is personal, descriptive, and evocative. Advertisers should also avoid using language that is boring, vague, or uninspiring.
6. Test and optimize: Finally, it's important to test and optimize the use of emotion in advertising to ensure that it is as effective as possible. This may involve testing different emotions, using different storytelling techniques, or using different visuals.
7. Use positive emotions: Positive emotions such as happiness, excitement, and inspiration can create a positive association with the product. This can lead to increased brand loyalty and repeat purchases.
8. Use negative emotions: Negative emotions such as fear, anxiety, and anger can also be used to sell products, particularly products that solve a problem. For example, a security company may use fear of theft to sell home security systems.
9. Show, don't tell: When using emotion in advertising, it is more effective to show rather than tell. Advertisers should use visuals, such as images and videos, to demonstrate the emotions they want to evoke rather than simply describing them.
10. Be authentic: Emotion in advertising should be authentic and genuine. Advertisers should avoid using fake or exaggerated

emotions, as this can lead to distrust and skepticism among the target audience.

11. Use humor: Humor can also be used to evoke emotions in advertising. Advertisers should use humor that is appropriate, relevant, and in line with the target audience's sense of humor.
12. Emphasize the benefits: When using emotion in advertising, it's important to emphasize the benefits of the product. This may involve highlighting the product's features, its positive impact on the user's life, or its emotional benefits.

By using positive and negative emotions, showing rather than telling, being authentic, using humor, and emphasizing the benefits, advertisers can effectively use emotion to sell products. Emotion is a powerful tool in advertising, and by tapping into the target audience's emotions, advertisers can create a strong connection with the reader and drive conversions.

Chapter 8

Writing Effective Social Media Ad Copy

Ad copywriting is not a one-size-fits-all approach. Different media formats, such as print, digital, and television, require different approaches to ad copywriting. In this chapter, we will explore the different media formats and provide tips for crafting optimized ad copy for each format.

1. Print ads: Print ads typically appear in magazines, newspapers, or flyers. Ad copy for print ads should be short and to the point, as readers often skim print ads. Advertisers should also use eye-catching headlines, images, and graphics to grab the reader's attention.

2. Digital ads: Digital ads, including display and social media ads, can appear on websites, mobile apps, and social media platforms. Ad copy for digital ads should be optimized for the platform and may include calls to action, such as clicking on a link or downloading an app. Advertisers should also use multimedia, such as images and videos, to increase engagement and conversions.

3. Television ads: Television ads typically appear during commercial breaks and are usually 30 seconds or 60 seconds in length. Television ad copy should be concise and memorable and include a strong visual component. Advertisers should also use attention-grabbing visuals, such as images, videos, and animation, to grab the viewer's attention.

4. Radio ads: Radio ads typically air during commercial breaks on radio stations. Ad copy for radio ads should be concise, memorable, and easy to listen to. Advertisers should also use sound effects, music, and vocal talent to make the ad more engaging and effective.
5. Outdoor ads: Outdoor ads, including billboards, posters, and bus shelters, are typically viewed from a distance and are designed to be seen in passing. Ad copy for outdoor ads should be simple, bold, and attention-grabbing. Advertisers should also use high-quality images and graphics to make the ad stand out.
6. Direct mail: Direct mail is advertising delivered directly to the consumer's mailbox. Ad copy for direct mail should be personal, targeted, and relevant to the recipient. Advertisers should also use high-quality images, graphics, and materials to make the ad stand out and grab the reader's attention.

Chapter 9

Writing Effective Social Media Ad Copy

Social media has become an increasingly important platform for advertisers to reach their target audience. With billions of active users on platforms such as Facebook, Instagram, and Twitter, social media offers a vast and diverse audience for advertisers to reach. However, with the increasing number of advertisers vying for attention on social media, it is becoming increasingly important for ad copy to be both effective and attention-grabbing.

When writing ad copy for social media, it is important to understand the unique aspects of each platform. Different social media platforms have different algorithms, demographics, and user behaviors, which can all impact ad copy effectiveness. Advertisers should also consider the length of ad copy, the use of images and videos, and the placement of calls to action.

Here are some tips for writing effective social media ad copy:

1. Keep it short and sweet: Social media users are often scrolling through their feeds quickly, so it is important for ad copy to be concise and to the point. Ad copy should be brief and focused on the most important message or benefit.

2. Use attention-grabbing headlines: The headline of an ad is often what determines whether or not a user will engage with the ad. Advertisers should use attention-grabbing headlines that are both informative and memorable.

3. Make use of images and videos: Social media is a highly visual platform, and images and videos can be a powerful

tools for grabbing the attention of users. Advertisers should make use of eye-catching images and videos that are relevant to the ad copy.
4. Test different calls to action: Calls to action are an important component of ad copy. Different calls to action may work better for different social media platforms and target audiences. Advertisers should test different calls to action to determine what works best for their ad campaign.
5. Target specific demographics: Social media platforms allow advertisers to target specific demographics, such as age, location, interests, and more. Advertisers should use this targeting information to create ad copy relevant to the target audience.
6. A/B test ad copy: A/B testing is a powerful tool for optimizing ad copy on social media. Advertisers can create multiple variations of ad copy and test which variations perform best, allowing them to continuously improve the effectiveness of their ad campaigns.
7. Match the tone of the platform: Different social media platforms have different tones and styles. For example, Instagram is often seen as a more visually-focused, creative platform, while LinkedIn is often seen as a more professional and business-oriented platform. Advertisers should match the tone of the platform they are advertising on to ensure their ad copy is both appropriate and effective.
8. Use humor: Humor can be a powerful tool for engaging users on social media. Advertisers should consider using humor in

their ad copy as long as it is appropriate and relevant to the target audience.
9. Make use of social proof: Social proof, such as customer reviews and testimonials, can be a powerful tool for building trust and credibility with the target audience. Advertisers should consider incorporating social proof into their ad copy to build trust and credibility with the target audience.
10. Utilize dynamic creative: Dynamic creative is a tool that allows advertisers to automatically optimize their ad copy for different target audiences and platforms. Advertisers should consider using dynamic creative to optimize their ad copy for different target audiences and platforms to ensure their ad campaigns are as effective as possible.

By following these additional tips, advertisers can further enhance the effectiveness of their social media ad copy. By understanding the unique aspects of each platform, targeting the right audience, and using the right tools and techniques, advertisers can drive better results and reach their target audience more effectively on social media.

Chapter 10

Measuring the Success of Your Ad Copy

In order to be truly effective, ad copy must be able to generate measurable results. Measuring the success of your ad copy is essential to understand what is working, what is not working, and how you can improve your ad campaigns going forward. In this chapter, we will examine the key metrics and tools you can use to measure the success of your ad copy.

Metrics to Track:

1. Conversion rate: This is the most important metric for measuring the success of your ad copy. Conversion rate measures the percentage of users who take the desired action after viewing your ad, such as making a purchase, filling out a form, or downloading an app. A high conversion rate indicates that your ad copy effectively communicates your value proposition and motivates users to take action.

2. Click-through rate (CTR): CTR measures the number of clicks your ad receives as a percentage of its total impressions. A high CTR indicates that your ad is relevant and engaging and that users are interested in learning more about your product or service.

3. Bounce rate: The bounce rate measures the percentage of users who leave your landing page immediately after clicking your ad. A high bounce rate can indicate that your ad copy and landing page do not match or that the user is not interested in what is offered.

4. Cost per action (CPA): CPA measures the cost of each action taken in response to your ad. This metric is important because it provides a direct measure of the return on investment (ROI) generated by your ad campaign. A low CPA indicates that your ad is driving more conversions per dollar spent, which is a good sign that your ad copy is effective.

Tools to Use:

1. Google Analytics: Google Analytics is a free and widely-used tool for measuring the success of ad campaigns. This tool provides detailed insights into user behavior on your website, such as conversion rate, bounce rate, and CTR.
2. Ad tracking tools: Ad tracking tools, such as AdWords and Facebook Ads, allow you to track and measure the performance of your ad campaigns on specific platforms. These tools provide detailed data on impressions, clicks, conversions, and other key metrics, making it easy to measure the success of your ad copy.
3. A/B testing tools: A/B testing tools, such as Optimizely and Visual Website Optimizer, allow you to test and compare different versions of your ad copy. This is a valuable tool for determining which elements of your ad copy are most effective and making improvements accordingly.

Additionally, it's important to remember that measuring the success of your ad copy is not a one-time event but a continuous process. As your target audience and the market evolve, you need to regularly assess and adjust your ad copy to ensure that it remains effective. This can be achieved through regular monitoring of your ad performance, conducting surveys and focus groups, and staying up-to-date with industry trends and best practices.

Another important aspect of measuring the success of your ad copy is identifying and addressing any potential roadblocks to conversion. For example, if your conversion rate is low, you may need to reassess your value proposition, headline, or call to action to ensure that they are clear, compelling, and aligned with the needs of your target audience.

Finally, it's important to understand that measuring the success of your ad copy is not just about achieving a high conversion rate or a low CPA. It's also about understanding the needs, wants, and motivations of your target audience and using that information to create ad copy that connects with them on an emotional level. By doing so, you can build trust, establish a loyal customer base, and create a sustainable, long-term ad campaign.

In summary, measuring the success of your ad copy is a critical component of any effective ad campaign. By tracking key metrics, using the right tools, and continuously adapting to the needs of your target audience, you can create ad copy that drives not only results but also establishes a strong, emotional connection with your target audience.

Chapter 11

Tips and Tricks for Writing Ad Copy That Works

As you delve deeper into the world of ad copywriting, you'll find that there are many tips and tricks that can help you create ad copy that truly resonates with your target audience. In this chapter, we'll explore some of the most effective strategies for crafting ad copy that drives results and stands out from the crowd.

1. Know your target audience: One of the most important things you can do to create effective ad copy is to have a deep understanding of your target audience. This means researching their demographics, interests, and buying habits, as well as their pain points and what they hope to gain from your product or service. The more you know about your target audience, the better positioned you'll be to craft ad copy that speaks directly to their needs.

2. Write a clear, concise headline: Your headline is the first thing your target audience will see, and it's often what determines whether they'll keep reading or move on to the next thing. Your headline should be clear, concise, and attention-grabbing, and it should communicate the main benefit of your product or service.

3. Make a strong value proposition: Your value proposition is the main reason someone should choose your product or service over your competitors. This is your opportunity to clearly communicate the benefits of your product, so make

sure it's concise, compelling, and differentiated from what others are offering.

4. Use emotional appeals: People often make buying decisions based on their emotions, so it's important to tap into this by creating ad copy that elicits an emotional response. This can be achieved through storytelling, using persuasive language, and highlighting the benefits of your product or service in a way that resonates with your target audience's values and desires.

5. Make a strong call to action: Your call to action encourages your target audience to take the next step and convert. It should be clear, concise, and positioned prominently within your ad copy. Make sure your call to action is specific and tells your target audience exactly what you want them to do (e.g., "Buy now," "Sign up today," etc.).

6. Use social proof: Social proof is the idea that people are more likely to do something if they see others doing it. You can tap into this by highlighting customer reviews, testimonials, and other forms of social proof within your ad copy.

7. Test and refine: Finally, it's important to continually test and refine your ad copy. This means experimenting with different headlines, value propositions, calls to action, and other ad copy elements to see what resonates most with your target audience. Continuously monitoring your ad performance, using split testing, and incorporating feedback from your target audience can help you make data-driven decisions about changes to your ad copy.

Chapter 12

Conclusion and Final Thoughts on Ad Copywriting

Writing effective ad copy is a crucial component of any successful advertising campaign. It requires a deep understanding of your target audience, the ability to craft compelling headlines, and the know-how to write body copy that converts. By incorporating emotion, creating a strong call to action, and using different media formats, you can effectively communicate your unique value proposition and sell your products.

Measuring the success of your ad copy is also essential, as it allows you to make data-driven decisions about what is working and what needs improvement. In this chapter, we covered a wide range of topics related to ad copywriting, from the importance of a unique value proposition to writing effective social media ad copy.

In conclusion, ad copywriting is an art and a science, and the more you practice, the better you will become. As you continue to learn and grow, remember to always keep your target audience in mind and strive to create ad copy that resonates with them and drives results. The tips and tricks we discussed in this chapter should provide a solid foundation for your ad copywriting journey, but there is always more to learn and discover. Keep experimenting, and never be afraid to try new things! With time and dedication, you will become a skilled ad copywriter and an invaluable asset to your organization.

www.ingramcontent.com/pod-product-compliance
Lightning Source LLC
Chambersburg PA
CBHW050241220526
45465CB00017B/853